CSU Poetry Series XLII

Jan Freeman

HYENA

Cleveland State University Poetry Center

Acknowledgments

Grateful acknowledgment is made to the following publications, in which some of these poems first appeared.

The American Poetry Review: "Mother Waken," "Green Trap," "Broken"
The American Voice: "Comedian," "Song for the Red-Haired Widow," "Hyena," "Her Oddity," "Mountain Rhyme"
American Writing: "From the Pictures I Could Track You"
5 A.M.: "Come Home"
Ms.: "Connections"
The Women's Review of Books: "Morning," "Summer Melody"

"Autumn Sequence" was first published in a longer version by Paris Press, Northampton, Mass. (1993).

I would like to thank Robin Becker, Nina Cassian, Tory Dent, Sharon Olds, Fred Smock, and Ruth Stone for their useful advice and guidance during the many evolutions of this book. I thank Edgardo Bianchi, Kathy Loesch, and Siena Sanderson for their generous support and encouragement. To my family and to the memory of my grandfather, Philip Freeman: I thank you for the foundations that made writing these poems possible. Many thanks to the Virginia Center for the Creative Arts, the Wolf Pen Writers Colony, the Helene Wurlitzer Foundation, and the Ragdale Foundation for their gracious gifts of time, which enabled me to write many of the poems in this collection. Thank you to Ellie Byrom-Haley for her fine cover design. Finally, I thank the editors of the Cleveland State University Poetry Center, especially Nuala Archer and Leonard Trawick, whose valuable suggestions and assistance helped to make these poems into a breathing book.

Manufactured in the United States of America

ISBN 1-880834-06-5

Library of Congress Catalog Card Number: 93-71914

Funded Through
Ohio Arts Council

727 East Main Street
Columbus, Ohio 43205-1796
(614) 466-2613

Contents

For Gloria Zukerman, Maurice Hundley, and Kathleen Loesch. Through loss, risk. Then courage. Then power.

Hyena

The hyena has a happy heart:
hearts, hearts, many hearts.
The hyena has a happy heart.
At noon she seeks them,
at dusk she finds them,
at night she grabs them, bleeds them, eats them.
The hyena grins at the scent of a lame one,
one in mourning, one in pain, one barely breathing:
weak ones! weak ones!
Sometimes they fold themselves
into her jaws;
mama, they cry.
She swallows the flesh.
She loves the blood, the silky gestures and the scrub,
the matted hair, each forlorn whimper.
So what if the lions hate her.

I

Salome

I lounged in a lounge chair waiting for the sunshine,
the yellow line exactly between my legs
until the shiny car snapped my neck and jammed my head
on the silver bumper: my bloody head stuck to a brand-new bumper.
No way to pull it off, bloody head stuck to the bumper.
No way to pull it off. No simple muscle, simple suntan:
watch the car; here comes the car;
I waited for that bloody bumper.
Ten minutes passed on the dumb gray highway.
Poor driver can't look back; he drives fast so my head will fall,
arms miles away, arms, legs on the bloody road.
Who will pull the head from the shredded metal, place it on a soft pillow,
soft place, clean sheet, wrap the head in a clean white sheet
and place it sideways in a soft hole?
Stupid girl, lounging on a highway.
What kind of girl tries to push new steel? Stupid girl.
What makes the trucks go fast and the cars go fast
as they turn the bend, girl?
The moment I grew up I learned to smell around that bend:
here comes a clean car clean car
to pull my head from my lopsided shoulders.
The driver thinks he can settle it all with a little money and a little water
but it's not my blood or my empty look that doubles the attendants over,
keeps their dirty hands in their pockets:
nothing on my face will fit a favor, blood or payback;
they hate my hair and my crooked eyebrow.
I know where I am, ugly. None of their blowtorch talk can touch me:
no neck, no body in sight, no hands, no feet, no kick.
I left my useless self in the middle of the highway,
yellow line between my legs.
One eye shut, call me tender. One eye open, call me dead.

Split the Skin

Search for the mother,
search for the father,
oh lover, oh lover, the burden upon you.

The lamb snoozes through daylight,
sleeps through moonlight,
cannot know blue light;
the temperature winds between
partial and throughway.
Lie on top.
Even absence dozing flings panic:
I do not have resistance;
I have slit it in pieces;
I have broken it down.
I know the empty tub;
I know the clothes too tight;
I turn over and over.
I cannot stand closure.
Lie on top. Weigh me down.
Attach ropes. I cannot stand to feel the air.
Lie on top. My mouth must fit snugly, the breasts,
lie on top; I cannot shut my mouth.
My tongue sucks, a reflex,
my mouth, lie on top: I cannot stand to breathe.
Too much space, too much air.
Exert pressure, bear down.
Fill me up. Your body on top of my body;
your body inside of my body; let my body inside your body: lie on top.
This air too open, the space too wide: weigh me down. Let me in.
Lamb shorn from the skin. Lamb clipped: let me in, split the skin.
I need blood. Let me in. Too young, that heat, take me back:
I cannot breathe this air. Without air, lie on top, without air,
take me back, lie on top, without air, to that scarlet enclosure.

Comedian

for Robbie Tillotson

In drag Robbie tries to fool the Washington and Lee boys;
he gators in the beer flood on the floor at the bar at Sweet Briar.
He is a trickster.
He scored hundreds of points for his high-school basketball team.
He is not an ordinary queer.
He stutters and laughs hysterically in an extra-large jersey
and beautiful soft leather slippers.
I trace my snaps to filter the nausea.
He dies in the middle of the punchline.

Robbie painted portraits with branches on the edges
to clearly relate the internal structure behind the mask:
the face, the makeup, the glasses, the dress, the gloves.
Robbie painted masks everywhere but in the cradle of the eyes.
He left the eyes clean. He said so.

Do you penetrate?
Do you like the feel?
Do you infiltrate purposely or by accident?
Do you clip your cuticles carefully?
How often do you fear?
How often do you fear the virus?
Have you studied your list of lovers today?
Their list of lovers?
Their list of lovers?
Do you feel safe? Over easy? Overly easy?

When I am nervous, I shut mine.
When I am allergic, I rub mine red.
When I am quizzical, I tighten my upper and lower lids.
Without my glasses, I can see you more clearly now perhaps
than you can see me.

To die with shame.
To die with shame.
To die with the high-school basketball scores on the tip of the tongue,
so that words like swishy faggot won't stick like glue to you.
Yes, I know, I hardly knew him, hardly know you.

Yes, somewhere in here is an egg of projection.
To die without speaking terrifies me.
To die with the masks still confused with the face below,
shocking and horrifying still even to those familiar, deep down,
    deep down;
to die like that.

Quilting, he said.
We sew, we sew, we stitch ourselves until we don't know
ourselves and the quilt is always easier to see,
even with each blade or fin, each wire or coat hanger or
the sharp heels of the high heels from Blackbottom tucked into the surface,
    the soft blanket.
Image and truth are not confusing;
they are simply changeable by the minute.

During the last three weeks, he only read biographies of celebrities;
he slept with a bag of chocolate bars beside him in his bed
and a bottle of cooking sherry on his night table.
He sweated privately and kept his huge feet covered.
No one knew he was unpeeling himself so quickly;
no one knew he dumped his food in the dumpster every night quietly.
He played the self-help tapes on his Walkman; a master of discretion,
he kept us laughing. Our laughter heaved from our bellies
when he told his stories.

Oh mother, hold him closely. Hold him gently so that now he can weep,
die with regret, die with the open fear of the dying,
or nervously tell more funny stories.
Hold him gently mother. Perhaps he was shamed.
Perhaps he was shamed, mother, always.

Green Trap

Dusty, cat hair, sneeze
incessantly: green trap. Laundry green
trap. Who's on the bottom? I'm on top:
green trap. Suck the nipples: green trap;
keep the doors locked.
Under the anthem: green trap.
Below oxygen, above sky: green trap.
Less than a milligram of fat per serving:
green trap. Follow from car to car: green trap.
Whose heart more green than this?
Whose life more green than this new sprout, early May day.
What flattens or sings or protrudes less round?
I stand in the doorway.
What green eye from the copper beech
stares at us: above, below.
I know those squints. I know
culpability: flash flagrant grandpa,
one more lover for Whitman;
I remember the young men splashing in the river.
Whose eyes peer now at the smooth pale forms?
If we keep it abstract then we can live with it more easily.
Your judgment now simply part of my melody in this green trap.
In this green trap the leaves unwrap,
the ground warms, and the dogs refuse to come inside;
in this green trap, higher than a house, deeper, more pungent than any
        stained crucifix:
we skip and swing our arms together
in this green trap: genuflect, my limbs can't hold me up:
gravity means on your back in the hem
of birds awake and the shutters gentler than before
and the buttercups shining their yellow to the pansies
all morning and ready to go higher or steeple
we run to the stream and stand beneath willows;
in this green moment all love is lures, all arms are fence,
all language a sorrowful hole in the ground
preparing our green hearts for absence.
In this green trap the shoulder leans over and the robins cover
and the dogwoods flower as the cherry blossoms drop their clots:
in this green trap, the plastic is laid;

in this green trap, I cut holes for the parsley;
in this green trap, all signs point inward:
a simple glass pitcher with four matching cups.
Who loves who more in this green trap?
Too many mixing bowls, too many arms risen: take me in take me in.
In this green trap, that much hunger;
in this green trap, every wage matters;
in this green trap, the cat hates all collars;
in this bright room beside how many brilliant trees,
ivy nearly silver and the rose of Sharon green now,
the breeze smoother and the shadows lighter:
I accept the quavery voice of the mother;
I accept the erratic sorrow of the father;
I accept the departures of the brother and the sister
and the anger of the sister nearby.
The angel-white dogs will always love me and the cat
as long as canned fish matters, and the green trap is warm
while the birds racketeer; any season breathes delivery,
I love the color:
unhinge the fence, knock a hole through the wall;
and this green trap is as safe as any home.
In this green trap:
in this green trap:
who saddles the entrance and lassos the exit
and sees the faces of new friends around the bend
beyond the stream:
this green trap is fertile and generous:
I call you over and I lie beneath,
I call you over and I lie beneath,
I whisper your name in the pillow case,
all traps are the same: I love whose name?
Keep the door unlocked: I love whose name?
Keep the windows open: I love your name.
Every love is the same: this blanket of movement
safer than the trumpeter shining our portrait
in the instrument: distorted.
In this green home, a concert of voices
and bodies resembling the subtlest movements: head turn or foot tap;
in this green home in this green home in this green trap
happy as a smiling house covered in moss and soft as fur
in this green home green heart green head

happy as a green lark trapped in a burgundy bed: that fertile, this trap
and that safe this trap and that familiar this trap
all arms and legs, all casement and casualty
in this green trap, all hem all thread
all glass blue or yellow in this fragile green trap
woven in my green wire, charged beyond safe overdrive,
green trap green trap, infant to old maid,
yes, old enough to know let go
in this green trap where the breath began
and the eyes saw who as the head rolled sideways
in this green trap this trapped one always
in any season
love was first
never abandon.

Mother Waken

She tells me she rubbed the bellies of the newborn cats
and the little legs stretched
and I dreamed I had a baby.
I dreamed that birthing was not painful.
I dreamed I had a baby and I carried that baby with me like a doll.
The six a.m. sky is as soft as sleep.
Part of the dream was running but part of the dream was peace.
The bronze headed grackles cover the green lawn.
Nearly all of the yellow grass is gone.
The rain is falling down.   .
Sleep tunneled part of the moon.
I carried that baby with me from shop to shop.
I laid that baby down to nap beside me on the floor.
That baby, more delicate than any fish or body of feathers,
knew every pinch I had in mind.
That baby knew my language, knew me sprung from a heart;
that baby from the sea in me, still small but already grown,
knew every neck I wanted to own,
knew how strange to grow in two small rooms,
and she hardly cried, even in that tiny palm of space,
even unable to place her father and knowing that I couldn't place
        him either,
knowing she came from gentleness and that bitter thought could not stand
in a room so filled with talcum and the oily scent of scalp.
The baby on her back in a brand-new pair of pajamas
allowed herself to be watched,
and I lifted the small body and remembered I had to feed it.
I held the peach head next to my ordinary breast
and she started to suck and the milk was there
and she sucked and she sucked like a reflex
and I propped her in place.
I wanted to show that baby to everyone I knew.
That baby was my surprise. That baby was my magic.
That baby pulled me out of a hat.
Our heads were warm and our skin was flushed,
and she suckled and I crooned, and half of my womanly fear left.
I held my elbow and rocked my arm.
That baby knew what she could count on;
she knew my loyalty.

The sky openly offered its eye.
The rain pressed down down,
and buds, pinched but soft, were covering many branches.
I held her in place until the blood seemed to stop
and my fingers tingled and lost sensation.
I held her with dim light on a bedsheet and rain in every window
and spring rising up from the earth, spring changing every color,
spring, that warm wet air, woke me slowly
and I put her down, I let her go.

Connections

My teeth are going tick tick tick.
I can't stand women who dismiss women.
My teeth are thinning and forming points.
I can't stand I can't stand women who want to be like men,
who dress like them and walk and posture arrogance like them.
Like some men, not like all men.
And yet, I can't stand too much delicacy.
I can't stand excessive vulnerability.
I can't stand looking at those faces, those faces taped with restraint.
I hate that look, those eyes, those eyes that push out and try
to catch you at the same time. I hate that.
There is no sensuality in porous pain, no real visage
other than the nerves, the nerves, the nerve endings,
spastic or paralytic, no giving, just that greed.
It eats me. Those kinds of women, those kinds of lives on those faces
make me vicious, vicious and hungry for damage, hungry for infliction,
yes, that kind of cutting, the close to murderous cutting you read about
in newspapers, that kind of veteran rampage which battles excuse,
and uniforms exonerate, that kind of strangulation, that kind of beating;
those faces make me strong, make me strong when they are not
      reflections,
when they are familiar but safely without a certain kind of resemblance.
Women fill me with lust and gentleness and the sense of starvation
when they turn to pools before my eyes, when they turn to places
to float on and hide in, they turn me, some of them turn me into
my infancy, and others turn me into a raging monstrous head on legs
filled with roars and loud and hardy belts of laughter and weeping,
weeping uncontrollably.
What am I what am I what am I without conflict?
And what are you? What type are you? How easily can you identify?
What is that resting by your head? What texture do you lust for?
Where are you standing? What are you made of?
This mileage wraps me tighter than a cast.
How close am I to you?

Painting the Dead

I
Green hair
triangular face
blue night
stars in the night
yellow face
green hair
less light
less man.

II
She is a bloody woman:
red body,
the air around her red
apple skin.
A red line around the red mouth,
bloody red cap,
her red eyes trapped in this red world
half on fire.
Shut or not, she pulls the hood.

III
This is not Joan, blue hat:
leaves above her lungs provide
the oxygen she needs.
Joined and drugged:
never dead the green leaves,
poppies hold her stance.
Eyes hammered still
behind the rim and knotty edge as
outside engines tear the surface
and she begs to be left alone.
The fire of speech is killing her,
the fumes, the light is nothing but
a net to keep her deeds
within good taste
and she is reasonable.

IV

Risen from the pink water
mouth shut
eyes, the lids shut with two blue thumbprints,
clavicle risen
hair or hat:
she is a head risen out of the sea
a shoulder, a neck;
she is a mouth pinned shut
and safe.

V

The world is a dull vision. Sheep beside her, head tipped:
an early radiation, head on fire, hands clasped before her.
If she can hold them in place the sheep will stay where they are placed
her feet will stay where they are placed if she is silent.

VI

Hardly an eyebrow on her;
a foggy face, hair all armor,
smiling devil behind her,
weeping woman beside him.
She needs an angel to carry her out.

VII

The window opens, a monkey
runs to a crevice to hide;
she feels the skin under her arm,
she sees the throat:
from the neck down, colorful,
she is a red mess; under the neck:
a scar, a line of thin hair, peach
broken under the tree;
beside the bed in a great heap
radishes lie, pink and white;
monkeys run crevice to crevice.
Slippery stones, rain, snow;
shut the window.

Transformation

At first I loved the beautiful bird
for the color of its feathers and the shape of its head
and its impressive size, its boldness.
Then just as I was leaving the comfortable restaurant
with my mother and her crutches,
the maitre d', dressed like a pinwheel, speaking in a flurry,
mentioned the bird was homeless, no mother loved it;
and I pitied the beautiful bold bird,
and I did not mind that it followed us as we walked.
I called attention to the green and yellow and red palette
that made its feathers such a sight:
a bird like a western bandana, like a tropical cocktail,
a beautiful bird.
So I walked with my mother and the bird followed at a distance,
then suddenly paced its flight closer, and we began to walk faster
and my mother moved quickly with her crutches
and the bird moved heavy as a cable car, its shadow a room around us.
We got to the top of the hill,
looked down,
and at the foot of the hill a long cage the length of a block-long
        sidewalk stood,
and I said to my mother, let's run let's run into the cage close by,
that bird is following us too closely; that bird is getting greedy;
that bird may be more dangerous than pretty.
So we ran, my mother with her crutches and I beside her and breathless
entered the cage just in the nick of time.
Just in the nick of time we locked the bird out.
With the bird on one end flapping we rested in the long cage
and the longer we sat the worse I felt: poor motherless bird;
until out of the clapping of someone's hands upside down in the
        dogwood tree
the bird turned into an aardvark.
An aardvark, angry, with a nose like a pale peach, a nose long and peachlike,
and my mother with her crutches and I beside her worried how long we
        might stay in that cage.
That cage was stunning and fit for a lion tranquilized and shipped
from a jungle to a petting zoo. We cherished it. That cage saved our skin.
Such fruitiness, such radiance, in such an ordinary place added a bit
of scenery to the manicured lawns of the town.

Soft as pimento I am the daughter.
Yes, I am the daughter gentle as pimento.
The long nose poked its bit of terror through me.
Now the bold bird sings in the aardvark.
The crutches prop my mother.
Shapeless colors frighten the evening, unpeel the obsidian resting
beneath the slope of the hill.
On brief vacations, intervals, the aardvark lounges behind the trees,
unleashes the bird to flap its sorrow.
Let me in let me in, sings its madrigal voice,
a macaw, a transvestite, feathers askew. Poor bird.
Occasionally, the wire mesh widens to windows;
a silver eyelash shifts behind a curtain, a sea enters,
everything high and low, blue; one feather balances dry.
The cage rises: from the bird's song, one bleeding bust, a gray shelf
grown into its neck, one flight framed on a wall beneath it.
What beautiful bird sings from the aardvark's belly?
Who watches the beauty, ignoring the crooked pose across the cage?
What fear is accurate?

Inheritance

No splint am I, no gentle source.
No arm around arm without tourniquet.
I cannot move beyond an unpeeled face
without swooning from the merciful.
Jagged words rise out of me
even with each eye averted from the open motion
that sickens me faster than the sea.
Sister.
No street exists without steps clicking behind for some show of assurance.
I can't eat a meal without a silent plea hooked through my spine.
I am frozen from signage.
Less or more than what I was at six,
I force myself to stare in her direction.
Invisible or visible, she is everywhere.

There is nothing melodic in the silver loops my anger leaps through.
Such revulsion: each wave of empathy or dismissal,
the brown-haired head and blue eyes she trailed me with.
How gentle I prove my spirit to detest so fiercely
any gesture revealing a soft core.
She is the one who can't stop talking.
She is the one who kissed for favors.
But this is not a carnival town. This is not a house of blatancy.
The overt is forbidden.
Imbalance, unacceptable, I reveal the complex design of wires,
my own electrical formula before dissolution:
Don't touch me.
Don't touch me.
I can't tolerate touch without sexual visitation.
Touch is provocative.
That was clear from the start,
and spoken love is demeaning as physical affection.
It is cheap and cheap blooms darkly.
I tried to be good; then good swirled into dizziness,
it swirled into nausea;
and she was bad, my sister was bad, and that didn't save her;
it kept her hungry.
This was never intentional.
From the start it came from protection,
the hands and the voices of our parents' parents.

Dead branches on a vital tree.
Burnt grass on a green lawn.
Brown spots in a green sea.
Black prints through a white sky.
This sister is my doom: she shows a map tracing my incapacity
for the accessible; love, it would never be easier.
And still, closure lines my face.
Still I am splayed between acceptance and aversion to the hands,
innocent, to the hug, publicly common, terrifying,
every occasion calculated, uncomfortable, untrained.
If we could fix each other —
but already we are past that mirror.

A green lawn as inviting as a green sea.
A white sky as restful as a white room.
The hand beneath the plowed field
dark as the hand caught in the burning prairie.
As frozen as I may seem, I am more brittle with any sign of intimacy.
But here, I have snatched a lineup of intelligent contestants;
they are beneath the clothes that shield me.
Choose one, my sister, or I will choose her for you.
I have names for them all.
I have met them and interviewed carefully.
I have timed each contact.
Each one fills me with envy.
They hold and hold, and never think anything of it.

I Wandered in the Palm Sleep Held for Me

I wandered in the palm sleep held for me.
Birds peeped above the sagebrush the next morning.
Dorothy hunted prairie dogs, death dogs;
Tres Piedras in the distance, nearly all of the sky, cloud.
The spirit wished wished beside my head;
it pulled me toward the north wall.
I could not speak;
I could not move.
The road ended at the turn; I could not see
beyond the turn; up from the green ground, blue mountains,
crows proved dimension, east west.
The spirit by my head: wish wish toward the north wall.
I could not speak;
I could not move.
Sky pasted shadows on the mountains, and her pale light.
Bodies melded into mountains, giant limbs in the distance.
There was so much pressure,
but not from mountains.
The stray, part coyote, howled with the pack all night;
they strung the mesa with their high moans;
the stars, that hazy Milky Way, slipped kisses in the breeze
above the rooftop: in the morning, every adobe golden;
the mountains: touch me, place your hand here;
the sun a silver coin behind the clouds.
Always frightened by the spirit,
I could not move;
I could not speak.
Mesa covered with sage, chamisa, cacti, foxtail,
one crow above the mountains.
When I turned, the road led back to town:
shops, tourists, people I might recognize.
The night before, the dream of choking:
my throat filled with the gummy substance,
my fingers down my own throat: breathe, speak.
I am that frightened of my mother's dying.

Summer Melody

The sky is as heavy as a biker's boot
and shiny as the biker's chain.
The field is as bright as a biker's tattoo,
the deer are as constant as a biker's refrain.
The road is as sleek as a biker's bike,
the fence is as crooked as a biker's might,
and I am happy to be home tonight
away from the bastards' claim;
away from their force and the voice on my neck,
away from that field, so large,
away from the men as they played with their knives,
and my young-girl pleading
and the faces of gristle
and the hands of oil
and the night in the back of that rust-colored van
and the shame on the road I walked as I walked home
with the blood in my shoe and my toughness ground down.
Oh, this evening is as peaceful as memory,
and a quiet mind, what luxury
when the biker's hold is as wide as his turf and his turf is wider than
        the noose he swings,
wider than the trail of hair he cuts,
wider than the sky's tranquility,
and stronger than my own stupidity for thumbing a ride
when I should have walked home, but craved some beer and muscle.
I was driven to that field with seven young Pagans
where I learned what to fear effectively
and yes I have feared them since.
For as hard as I try I cannot let them go,
so that even the landscape becomes them,
and each murderous story that swelled that night
locks me into its rubber casing;
and my legs are too weak to run from them
and they love every weakness shown to them.
The fields are as open as they stretched my legs open
and I am happy to be here tonight, nineteen years away.

Pandora's Seduction

Pandora's box is lined with eggshells ground into fine white powder.
One minute I'm in it; one minute I'm trying, in a wig and high heels
and a crimson suit, to unlock it with a clothespin from the outside.
Disguise is magical; it is a magical and creative pastime.
I am a new mistress, a regular seamstress;
I dress to your specifications if I can figure them out and they're feasible.
I am a woman of pharmacology. I am a witch. I am a blind student
    follower.
I am a poser. I take several in the course of a day and weave them into
    a view.
I travel with a stand-up mirror. Do you?
I like to pose naturally and as carefully as a reflection painted, written,
    and merchandised.
Evenings, I like to be seen. I dress like a meal and offer myself to the cook.
Her accent eats me. She tells me everything is lovely and seasoned
    carefully.
She always keeps a jar of turmeric with her.
She is *cordon bleu*, her left buttock tattooed with a piece of kale.
She is delicate and green.
Oh cook, oh cook, I adore you with or without your sauces.

I never dance. I never dance because it ruins the disguise.
A hula girl with skirt and top is all I want.
You know, the kind you push beneath the feet to make her twist and arch.
All women should have boxes like these to stand on.
What fun I'd have watching the ladies sway and tilt
instead of talk talk talk, boring me blue.
Sometimes I love apparatus.
Sometimes I love what you can do with a few springs and a pole.
Hallowed observation places buds on trees.
Try it out on your friends.
They will bloom in two weeks if you keep the heat high and their
    feet damp.
I adore plants. Do you?
Do you love the green leaves and the delicate stems?
Do you like to lie down on them? I do.
I like to drag my body over and over whatever is beneath me.
I use my tongue and my arms at once.
Is it you, is it you, is it you I feel? Or is it me?

Are you skirted? Are you scarfed?
Are you rhythmically reaching to meet the moon?
She is winged tonight and painted green like a jester;
her bells ring tonight as the violins play.
She dons magic tonight and she bellows the score.
Are you with me tonight as my shoes tie themselves temptingly?
Each lace swears it traces empathy around a sympathetic heart.
Is it you that my shoes refer me to, or is it the one who sits beside you
in the glass with wire in the shape of a smile sewn through her neck
to remind her of the sheltered luck she's had?
Is it true that we live for these moments?
Is it true that your feet meet me more than half way?
Is it true that we met in a mirror one day in June, in June,
in that fated month of weddings?

This earth is lonelier than suicide.
Perpendicular we try to ignore it while we straddle each other
and discuss disease.
We stand like amateur fossils waiting for the day to fix us.
Some people collect us.
Composure is the key; reinstated, she swallows all the oxygen in the room;
revised, she lies blind as a cork.
If we burn the field in April will the roots survive?
If we fill one room with feathers will the birds return?
If we stack the marble peaches in a pyramid will they equal a tree?
I am dressed today.
I remembered the stockings, the panties, the sheer brassiere.
Do I need more than this? I like to show it all without taking hours
        to strip.
Rub a little rouge on. Nearly everybody does.
Don't be shy. Feel free to walk around me.
I ground everything inside smooth and powdery as eggshells.
This is my best disguise.

Are you in or out? Are you out or in? Are you in the box or out of the box?
I keep the clothespin where no one can find it. I am safe. I am safe.
Inside and outside I am safe with or without you. I am nearly sure of it.
I love my box, my mirror, and each beautiful reflection I find there.
Call me Pandora. I know where I came from.
I am as safe as a lemon and a yellow pear.
I am clipped like the arm of the aloe propped in the jar of water.

I am so relaxed I can cure anything.
I am as perpendicular as any human being can manage on a velvet cloth.
Ask any man who knows me. Ask any woman too.
Ask each of my relatives, judges from birth.
I measure each breath. I am limber occasionally.
I live with the sound of my wobbly voice,
and I wear my skin thin.
Yes, love, my hidden sugar love,
my stern love, my malleable love, my transient love,
my heart is like a billy club; my fear is immortal;
and I am fragile, sewn too tight with invisible thread.
Love, I am fragile even with language,
even with lines sunk from poles, lines resting in water, lines moving
        toward you.
I strip myself and wait for your inversion;
I wait for your medic team of affection.
Who are you? Which one are you?

As perpendicular as a lemon to a pear,
I am perpendicular to your understanding, but oh how I'd like to be
        parallel.
I am stilted, yes, by my own limitations, by my own desires.
I am in the box and out of the box,
in the box and out of the box at once.
This way I cannot leave myself behind.
This way you know just where to find me.
The nightfall empties my anxiety, it empties my illusions;
my name is made of iron loyalty;
she cannot come apart.
Are you good with a needle and thread?
Do you know the trick of careful stitchery?
Can you identify the softest pulse,
stroke the wrist to add some color,
rub the neck to loosen muscles?
Each of the walls has been whitewashed.
There is room for countless markings.
Pandora's box is so enormous a choir of friends can come with you.
Are you in or out?
When we find a head that's blown full speed, and the head finds a home,
and our arms intertwine,

and our lips stick together, and you see me as I am, and you
     do not disappear,
and the head spins, and the head spins faster,
and we compose each other, while we compose ourselves
maybe then my form will twist and swing and bend.
Maybe then each disguise will undress herself,
and you will see me as I am without.
Can you possibly deny me? Can you look away? Do you have
     that strength?

In disguise or out of disguise the stand-up mirror is essential.
Are you in or out are you out or in?
I like your look; I cannot move.
I like your smell; my legs won't walk.
If I could touch that square between your ribs . . .
Won't you come in?
I've lost my balance.
The mirror ripples my reflection; it threatens dissolution.
There are purple tulips on the tables. Won't you come in?
The box is softening.
You are laughing.
Laughter doubles you over.
My face melts like a rubber mask;
each disguise confuses.
Your laughter reels through the walls, through the glass,
through the pie I have placed on the counter for you for you;
oh won't you come in?
My name is history already; it slips past each eye of the construction
     workers.
My pride, my surety, is useless; it has turned on me.
My habits poke me; your laughter coats me; I am dizzy with sensation;
your laughter is a magnet; I cannot get away.
My box brings tears to your hands; your laughter spins me.
I like your mouth; I cannot speak.
I like your mouth; I cannot scream.
I like your mouth; I cannot weep.
What honesty will silence you?
You laugh so hard milk runs from your nipples, urine slides down your legs.
I was born in my box, my beautiful box, and now your laughter blinds me.
I forget my old fantasies. I have locked myself out.
I've lost my clothespin.

I tried to protect it; I buried it; now I can't find it.
The laughter bleeds me. Tell me an answer.
I played the jester for fun: I wanted your eye in my pocket;
I wanted your heart for my new collection.
I left what I loved and loved and loved as a game.
The seduction was an act was an act was a comedy act.
This air is terrifying.
My costumes hang on me; some squeeze me; nothing fits.
Your laughter chokes me. Your hands grab my hands, grab my waist,
    grab my head.
My eyes are afraid of your eyes.
My tricks have lit a fire. My beautiful box is burning.
I am out I am out I am out; I swear I am out.
Stop laughing please stop laughing.
Tell me an answer.
Where do I go from here?

II

A Story

She took a knife and cut
a square from my throat.
Love poured out of it:
over the sheets and the wooden floors,
on the walls and the clean white ceiling.
Light faded, leaves drifted from the branches
outside the window; cars passed below the window;
morning slid to afternoon, cunts slick
as the daylight shifted.
Capture this moment, I said to the knife;
and she carved an "X" under my left breast.
She carved another on the top of my right thigh.
One line, she whispered, across your body:
a tightrope, a balance beam, a barometer;
when you feel the edge, I will cut the skin of your neck.
That drunk dead passion: my nerves slept beneath her gaze,
hands twisted, our bodies jerked, then night cast shadows.
Fool's heart, the summer hissed,
while photos of an earlier life smiled from every surface.
Cut my eyes, I begged the knife; but her careful fingers lifted
the skin above my clavicle, pulled, the puppeteer, as my body opened:
feel me, and her brown gaze settled on the cast:
puppets hung from every door frame: such colorful costumes!
Bells and ribbons dangled from appendages,
smiles painted brilliantly on their tiny masks,
while chins and jowls poked past the decorations;
and gently with the tip of the knife
she fixed the folds and the stray threads.
Now morning light slid beneath the door frames;
it pressed its cheek against the windows.
More, she whispered, taste me
as I hung, smiling like a snapshot of a happy lover
and another woman knocked against the front door.
I dreamed the knife was humming, but she hummed as she wiped the blade.
Another leg to tickle, I whispered as I wakened.
Leaves spun before the windows: green, gold, bronze, spring.
I breathed deeply and recalled a day of magnets, declarations,
walks at sunrise, swims at sunset, smoking wires, the white gazebo.
How I love the empty ceiling.

Come Home

The veins of my wrists, my arms, green lines; fields turning,
thin strips poking grass on the highway dividing lines.
Left under your willful silence, my own stippled resource:
from this place beneath the window,
what altered sight may loosen the wavering walls,
whether you quiet my sleep or awaken me shouting, come home, come home.
My tribute to you: an open spectrum, twin clavicles.

Sister, watch the sky: as we pull our murderous words apart, the fantasies,
      the brief exposures,
I aim my vision at the stillness and slap my hands against the gravel.
These hands raw, all self-infliction. Sister, please, for each bent word upon
      the page
and each flat look from the picture frames, for the trickery of out-of-bounds,
for the lipstick and the legs, for the razors, the critical one,
braided head splitting laughter, all mockery, those lips out of reach.
Slip your clumsy body into another frame,
stack the stones, but love me always.

I break the legs of the elder doll;
without question, the younger doll, more graceful, more adept at speaking,
will now move faster from avenues uptown, state to state, soon out of sight.
Beneath the window, my torso propped in a box.
No tears, no reservation, this internment perfectly tender.
If you shut the lid I will sing when I see the light.
Blessed is the one who runs fastest away from cruelty.

Run fast from me, sister.
My parakeet voice may startle you in dreams,
but far from here, your heart is safe.
My magic wand is a knotted root, my muse, the body slightly out of reach.
Memorize our shapes before you separate.
Open open wide, whose love inside?

Pound the box with hammer and tacks,
dig a hole too deep for escape.
Bury this body, airless, no injury:
stamp the earth above my head:
your freedom, sister, in the warm spring air,
extra light, one hour, no scorn, no trading now:
all judgment dead.

Her Oddity

Her oddity was sometimes more than she could bear.
People stared at her.
They wondered how she could keep it up.
Her oddity often brought the melancholy out:
we love you, they shined.
She liked the fantasy:
she played the hair and the hands,
she had the wardrobe.
Her oddity was deeper than a blemish.
It wore her out sometimes.

Mountain Rhyme

Sorrow placed its tongue on my thigh.
Open up, Sorrow said, let me in.
Turntables swung the lyrics aside.
Little flower, they sang, *mein kind.*

She cuddles the dog and she coddles the dog.
She says she's in love, now, with the dog;
and I follow on walks or watch their eyes
as they tenderly touch what I once touched.

Let me in, said Sorrow. You're in, I said,
you're up to my neck, you're near my head;
you've filled my belly with a tear of lead.
It's good to be home, Sorrow said.

The Temperature of Tears

A flock of robins on the back lawn: the return of consciousness.
Old leaves blown by breeze hop like the rusty chests and dim gray backs.
Everything turning slightly,
everything lightening or darkening,
the sky mild,
the veins opening to free the weather, the gradual warming.
Oh, slow air, don't terrify.
The dreams are still ahead of the sleeping woman.
She must waken slowly.
She must know slowly what an open heart she lives in, this weather.
Taken gradually, covered in linen, the morning wraps her body,
her weather, around the prairie, over the lawn, she wraps the kitchen,
the gentle gentle heat drops and rises as she wakens.

Each window rattles against each window frame: the ambrosia of field,
    prairie, stream.
A controlled waking, so much more difficult than sleep,
the dream carries into the wreaths of spring; spring and dream,
    synonymous:
the undercurrent, weeds lifting, leaves unbending, the grass, the
    scrub grass,
the press upward, the timed waves of warm air.
An ominous weight, this weather unlatching,
the mind still clamped, controllable.
Weakness of weather softens and stops, then forces the gradual stripping,
the gestured unpeeling of dream as each eye opens.
Mottled light groggily leans on an elm tree, stump of the dying heart.
Yellowy branches waken to welcome the assonance of return.
Trees, grass, the nipple buds push from the ground;
the earth separates to let each sprout shift its weight upward against
    gravity.
The dream opens the slow breeze, the waking around the body,
that gradual dilation;
it hangs itself from each corner of the room.
The mouth opens remembering the morning,
and the eyes open gradually, not to miss the morning;
the stillness after the dream's immersion:
the dog bleeding, her white fur matted and stamped with blood;
the men are dying in the hole in the earth, the temperature hot,

the weather too hot, the dream shifts in the body's waking;
the dream's waking places the dream into a plane that the half-
    sleeping body
absorbs in her palatable language: the men shifting to dog,
the dog shifting to grass, the pinning, the unpinning, the alterations,
the spring unfolding in the dream, the dream unfolding in the change
    of weather,
each untouchable evolution in the voice, the air, the arms of the spring
    morning.

Early spring surprises, pungent, filled with sorrow;
early spring with the graves of the dream and the graves of the earth
shifting in the shifting temperature of air and grass and ground.
The ground shifts ground, the heat breaks,
and nothing, wherever she is, is as malleable as she demands.
She carries the creams, the scars and winter's tension
in her dry and powdery skin; her complexion clear, without resolve,
and the weather's shift presses finally into the structures she has formed
to protect herself from the dream's play of each revelation,
each transient statement, each heavy breeze.
Winter, so exacting, could not pull the sorrows from her;
they glint like mica packed in shale.

She is still so near safe darkness,
deep in the ground beneath the men, far from the red fur.
The woman's tears are nearly inaudible;
their temperature, the color of human bodies,
the color of dream, the colors of spring.
She lies on the bed,
the horsehair mattress as constant as anything she has ever known:
such firmness, such disorder beneath the waking body;
her body warm, the air already warm and waiting:
her body palmed and kissed by spirits of the dream that can't abandon,
the spring that has become her.
Everything far too delicate begs to be broken. Her life startles in
    abundance.
She turns and turns again, but nothing leaves her.
The air is marked with alteration, the season marked, the dreams are
    marked,
the woman: penetrable, impenetrable, on this third day of spring.

My Falling Father

In the center of the apple
a blue egg.
A shut eye:
in the tight blue egg
in the body of the apple
a line.
A chord reached into a man
tumbling down the Metro steps:
whose hands find him?
Train or laundry line, an envelope.
He opens his mouth.
In the apple body
against the table top
who knew what stopped?
Silk against the mouth top.
A voice could save him.
He went walking in the woods, dark;
he would not open his mouth;
the dog peered over the bridge,
leaning with her
over the edge: the top not too far,
the edge not too rough,
the water deep.
A gentle voice in an apple,
singing bird's spine.
The worlds open, the worlds snap shut,
the worlds dim, open into the body of an apple.
No light inside the apple: one blue egg,
air sweet, and one blue eye
filled with the descending shadow of my falling father.

Broken

At first it was a Nike, great wings stretched toward the North Star,
and then it was an arrowhead thrown through the sky.
It was after the double rainbow,
after the San Juan Feast Day,
the Buffalo Dance, the Comanche Dance
the children balancing feathers and bells
stepping left and right, the young girls
moving slightly.
The sky like landscape, history and geography
merged into one, the boxes of old pawn
and the heavy hands of the red-haired Indian.
After stories of East Texas,
drowned cousins, evening dresses,
it was a sky stretching forward and back,
white corn stew, watermelon juice.
My arms toward her, held back
the questions that we tossed like sagebrush blown left, right
or green stones tossed from the road onto the clay.
It was Wednesday, after the storm, the road sticky from rain.
Fingers covered with silver and green turquoise,
she was ready for all kinds of flight
and I sat beneath the sky calling the clouds the shapes I saw.
I was ready for nothing, afraid,
suddenly rootless, without friends, family
as if dropped from the pregnant dog cloud onto the mesa,
night before me, day behind,
my home, a house of cards blown over.
She needed nothing, took no gifts, took no pictures.
Sad mouth, sad stare: I shot them after her like arrows,
and she ran them through her brown hair.
Not turning back, not seeing me hold onto the wooden square
she rubbed her brown arms, then closed the heavy door.
I owned nothing but my dog. I was thirty-five, dependent on recognition;
and the clouds changed shape as quickly as I named them.

Ding Dong

I rang her doorbell and ran away.
I love you I love you I love you.
I could not look at the soft round face.
I love you I love you I love you.
Each gentle finger thin on the face
I wanted to touch, I wanted to kiss.
I ran to the door. I rang the bell.
I thought of the fingers. I thought of the face.
I heard her steps on the wooden floor.
I love you I love you I love you.
I bolted so fast I knocked the door.
I love you I love you I love you.
I knocked the door open and she stood there.
I wanted to capture her with my hair.
I twisted my braids and asked for the time.
She smiled and said, please come inside.
I looked at the face. I looked at the hands.
I looked at the lips that spoke to me;
the neck slipped in and so did the legs,
but I stood frozen on the stair,
and she touched my chin, she touched me where
I'd never been gently touched before,
but there was the door.
I love you I love you I love you, I cried
and ran away.

Song for the Red-Haired Widow

I
She is the woman who awakened me:
get up, shake your constraints down,
unbuckle your hair, love your mother.
On the front porch at midnight,
mattresses thrown down like pale shining fish
warm and white, the sheets still creased,
the folds marked deeply into the cotton skin.
Trees and hand-wide leaves all around the screens;
geraniums and petunias in baskets and pots
suspended from the roof, hung from rusty hooks;
my fingers held a book in place:
a gardening book, a book of birds.
Closely we woke that night amid the crickets, the cowbirds, each breeze.
Every surface in the kitchen, sticky in the morning;
spiders hung above the stove: love me, love me,
lend me eyes, eyes, floating breasts.

II
Once there was a widow.
I adored her.
I stood to seduce her,
slept to dream her,
sang to feel her,
wept to coddle her.
Pale, in bed, she lay for days;
trays and stories and flowers I brought;
but never the courage to lie on top.
If I had been as brave as that
what shrieks would have blossomed
from whose wax lips?
The planets aligned and realigned themselves
more easily; fields of neutrons;
whose bottom perched over a bowl
bled Saturn into urine?

III
Who loved her left her sprayed with wounds,
each incision, each burn rising in pale welts.

Who loved her learned to frame her:
head perched over desks and mantels in the ladies' homes: matron,
    sparrow.
June forever stuck in the robin's nest,
mockingbird, finch, finch, hawk, owl half over the mountain,
frozen in the headlights, masked as a rotted stump,
rose after moments of stillness,
flew, septic, into the woods.
In that summer of idolatry, how many holy moments?
What choices lay in the wings? Stay, fly.
And the widow, desire, far beyond reproach.
I do, I do; what rhymes resonated over the mountain road!
Woman, woman, veil stitched to the skin's shadows.
Night, a summer resolution:
wings wings, the simulation of flight.
If I had asked her, would she have answered?
How many widows in mourning or out fit in the palm while the
    other hand
spread, extended by a practical arm, conducts the words, heart, heart,
left unsaid: who loved her loves her still.

Hands or Were They Birds?

The tips of feathers could swirl or with that assurance
whisper themselves along the spine:
the language of touch moving along what junction?
There once was a woman who lived in an attic,
she lived in an attic, no light no sky.
She lived in an attic and painted the walls red;
she painted the walls red and slept in a blue bed
but never knew colors to match on the outside.
Those tender birds, tips of wings circling,
apples hanging, threaded with wire.
Hanging head, crooked but orderly:
the woman used powder to fill up the cracks;
she filled the gashes with orange peels.
Touch, a game of here I am,
she practiced living carefully:
feathers pointed, awake all night.

From the Pictures I Could Track You

With both hands she takes my feet.
With her arm she wraps my body from behind.
With her hand she rubs my left breast.
Her fingers long, she waves them over the skin.
With the center of her palm
she raises the nipple of my left breast.
I do not know her.
I cannot see her.
I cannot hear her.
I will not feel her.
Along my neck she moves her dry lips.
Over my shoulder her unclipped hair falls.
With one hand she tilts my chin up.
With one hand she rubs my belly.
With her hands she feels my legs.
Up and down she moves her hands.
With her face she touches my hips.
First the left hip. Then the right.
She moves her head. Hair trails in circles.
Back and forth, her hair in circles.
I do not know this woman.
I cannot see her body.
I cannot hear her voice.
I cannot feel her skin.
A waving body, this woman, amorphous.
This woman holds my body, splits it down the center.
She takes half of my body with her, my shadow, one shell.
Left with the pressure, I am lighter.
Left with her pressure, I will not forget.
Left with her pressure, which half is my own?
Left with her pressure, my hands feel the body.
Whose hand on my right thigh?
Whose mouth sucks the finger?
What thread pulls my voice box?
With two hands I grasp two feet.
I beg the arm that wraps this body:
give me one finger, I'll suck it to creases.
Give me one palm; my right breast is lonely.
Give me one hand; my hips are uneven.
Face, face, follow me home.

That Fallacy

Where is the home when the home is heart
and the heart is divided between two bodies?
Heart divided, lust and love;
heart divided, kiss me, feed me.
Whose home is mine in the morning, love,
when the pillow creases and the neck bends sleep;
when one hand begs here, and the other, touch me;
when one leg folds dream and the other, brace me?
Where is my home when longing breaks me:
one body teases, one body weeps;
when one mouth whispers and one mouth speaks
in normal tones of the home's demise?
Turn, slap the ground, spin, rise above, twist, listen
lovely face, listen solemn face,
I am moving in two directions at once
with nowhere to rest, with no room for sleep,
with no heart at peace; whose hands are peace
to fold around my head, my heart divided?
Shelter is a solid heart; shelter lost, whose home my home
as I move forward, then glance backward, turn around, retrace my steps?
What link, whose skin? My skin is tender; who calls tenderness a
        solid form?
Whose eyes my floor and roof? Whose back a desk, a bed, a kitchen table?

Swept With an Enormous Sadness

The afternoon dropped like a concrete mass
but the boxwood held me safely.
The moth balanced on your fingertip
then slowly crossed to mine.
I sleep remembering your palm cupped up;
the days pass more in dream than waking.

Morning

Between hedges, blend the bodies
over paths the bodies moving
between hedges through the fog
mist surrounds the bodies, heavy.
Light begins, the bodies lifting
mist is rising, bodies lifting
day begins, the skin is touching
mouths, the skin all fingertips
the arms, the boxwood hedge concealing
and one kiss, the mist concealing
as the heat begins and light begins
and day begins the bodies.

III

Autumn Sequence

It was always the child: hold me.
It was always the pillow, the palm.
Between words, what language I tried to learn.
Save me one last time: the room damp,
the carpet matted, the walls stained.
This dwelling now familiar.
It was only another story of reflection:
that body on the bench, that body on the dock;
that body barely touched this body.

I

No vestal virgins in bed tonight:
raze the broken, raze the sullen,
the longest scream I blemish the air;
every room spins this disarray.
Hold me, hold me, let loose, let me loose.
I have this stone, a pale pink song as representation;
this joining more than temptation, that language:
I am not crying come come, but hold me in the water, sister,
my skin, that refuge, blue now with the fire of your departure.

II

Banners fly, costumes, a parade,
this brilliant floral array.
If I tell you now, how fast would the drummers
beat their sticks on the dried skin surface?
If I permit any leaning, my head to drop down on any part of you,
will the banners pack the air with camouflage?
Between these seas that fall from me I recollect fire,
earth, confirmation, nerves, nerve endings.
Already I know this, out of control, one soft face, soft voice
and I am lost under the rinse:
what reel wraps around me without warning;
an automatic weapon empties my arms.
No language, love: this hunger scrapes every edge from this body.

III

I have been circling these days circling
while the salt builds, while everything in this landscape
turns to o's: the cows' brown eyes, brown pond to swim in,
the mouths of the women, the moon's o and the stars' small o's
bright in the holy black sky.
That small slick bird for one moment held
may shut whose opening heart, oh light, the water the place
for softness now: the hardest task this letting go.

Oh, what will I do in the silence?
What sounds may shatter the stillness?
Whose heart forms which loose shadow?
Whose heart, the raft in shallows
floating under the spinning leaves, the sky;
whose head rests, oh, my gentle spirit?
What ripples against the structure, more than the pain repeated.
Open, smile, close your eyes;
with slow uneven strokes I move beneath the lids,
my arms against each brown body.
Oh, my heart, to heal this sorrow —

IV

The stench of the rotten leaves, dead fish:
I stitch all openings shut;
who left her poison here?
Who baited the bed with kindness, with skin so soft each hand caught fire,
shattered the lenses of open wide.
Fatter than any heifer on these fields
my neck adores a painful slaughter;
what I swallow I reminisce; what I sharpen
nothing could be as bright, as practised in damage
as the need, that pretty package: bows, flowers, candle drippings.
What foolishness, what trickery, arms, hair.
I never learned the difference between comfort and appeasement.
Kiss me once.
Kiss me twice.
I never learned to trust or not to trust,
but always to anticipate the worst.
Every time I imagine two faces merged as they were
I know that in this space, surrounded by air, I am asphyxiated:
the oxygen lines my lungs with shards of glass.
The vial on the table: two brown eyes stare up from its bottom;
they never blink now, closure forbidden, I beg to blind them;
what they know of me any visionary would pack into a bag and leave.
I praise your absence, your silence.

V

I have begun to dream her
hands arms face face fingers mouth
I have begun to dream her love mouth lips
wide lips full wide eyes mouth teeth tongue
I have begun to dream her legs thighs hips
bottom belly I have begun to dream her mouth thighs breasts
belly thighs thighs neck cheeks brows I have begun to dream her
arms hands back hands thighs calves mouth neck breasts
wrists shoulders thighs mouth teeth tongue
I have begun to dream her heart mind mouth hands mind heart
legs arms neck face hair mouth open wider slick grinding into palms
soft slick labia I have begun to dream her hard slick clit fingers on the tip
fingers on the sides swell red clit fingers dipping in fingers over smooth
hole open slightly open wider gently fingers over walls breath blown over
hard clit breath blown slightly into tongue tip barely over hard slick
tongue more firmly over walls into open over base of the hard clit over base
of the clit back back into anus open firmly into breath blown lightly over tongue
lightly over hard clit tongue fingers deeply deeply tongue flat over fingers deep
in open deep in out deeper in out tongue back mouth sucking slowly harder sucking
firm clit harder fingers back in out in out slow circles slower one finger
on the anus open one finger slowly circle pointing tongue in the open circle slowly
slowly circle tongue moving deeper finger circling wide body lifting open wider
legs open wider lips moving gently over slickness over soft slick hard slick lightly
lips over fingers lightly fingers lighter tongue slowly tongue slower body
dropping slowly down body slowly legs folding lightly hand down slowly down
I have begun to dream her hair over forehead cheeks damp hips rest down I have
begun to dream her mouth slowly mouth lips on lips tongue against tongue I
have begun to dream her eyes on eyes mouth on mouth hands over hands
face against face legs over legs I have begun to dream her stop.

VI

She stood naked and talked about her legs and the bicycle and the pool
or was it poetry, naked she sat or stood I tried only to look at her face
my eyes pulled down to her breasts my eyes pulled down she talked of
light imaginative places, ideas and she was not shamed by her body as I
was shamed by my own she stood firmly on the floor and did not seem
to notice the childish reflex: every woman's body hold me hold me
hold me a woman's body naked here in the heat by the bench the steam
heavy from the showers hold me while she talked about
a beautiful lake and a red canoe and swimming on her back naked below
the eyes of summer visitors.

VII

In the middle of the afternoon, my hand on the bedspread,
my middle finger circling lightly over and around the nubs of fabric,
over and lightly over, raising your nipple, the longer strokes
lightly circling your clitoris over the labia, back and forth
on this white bedspread: this finger, this fabric, the sum isolation.

VIII

Where have I fallen,
swing wide the sequence.
Hook me from the weather
too gentle to handle, this Indian summer.
These colors: what mask do I wear
that winds me to sleep:
the lake, one massive body.
I lay myself down,
legs, arms spread wide as which membranes stretched?
If the sky leans down to take me
or press me into brown water
what peace might find eyes floating, high, low,
ravages this naming: the bars rise, the cage constructed,
I pace, for touch I heave against the steel bars, touch me
on the dock, body locked to the wooden planks, home or away,
        no green cove,
no fountain, no outage: soon soon; the useless invocation pushes
my back through whose rotted planks, soon soon my arms will lose
sensation frozen in brown water, yellowy reflections, like oil, covering
every trace of my soon soon emancipation; what pleasure to waken
what loves every dullness, this monster, ravenous, stamps remnants
into grassy lawns, my permission granted, every color annihilated:
who lifts and walks shuts down all placidity.

IX

Pacing through the giant heart, the beat, beat,
her face was older, close, eyes, brown eyes and lips so soft I could not
press myself hard enough, that face, that close, and away away,
while we kissed our mouths too dry, while we kissed and our hands
moved along whose protection?

X

She left as the heat dropped off:
spring, summer;
what assurance of return?
The windows break from the pressure:
only warm weather may sing her head tipped sideways.
Soon soon; how many years pass?
Beneath my neck my rattling heart, my breasts;
open your sleeping mouth, Persephone, let this nipple
fit between your tongue and teeth.
Suck me hard, suck me gently,
Persephone, this winter will be bitter:
frozen limbs everywhere.
This shifting far too bitter: I dream you on sidewalks
passing, I dream you in passing cars, I dream your absence
corn, wheat, green, my friend, your absence and then force feeding
the four tires off on a strip of highway at night.
I dream you sucking this body awake, spring, summer, morning:
the broader the better,
the wetter the wiser,
more tender, potential,
the heat, my skin,
what exchange, your hands,
can pinpoint, oil,
one tongue licking
whose lifeline clean?

XI

All afternoon, silver webs float
past the window all afternoon
I wait, the dryness runs my heart like a line
of caps shooting off off each dead leaf
I wish into a bird I cannot stop:
the shadows reach the window;
time is out out running out. The shadows.
I know I cannot shift these alterations back,
such tiny pockets, each occurrence,
and a breeze turns the dead leaves over.

XII

I hold my hand over my mouth;
this way I keep the show secure.
No teeth today;
water water soft the fire:
this body, here, durable.
A tin plate carved with stars,
my shield; every flock against the view
shuts the clouds down.
No room for three in the space of one palm:
too many loves break the pot.
My hands, my saviors, phoebe phoebe:
if the shaking stops, will the bottles
break or blossom?

XIII

Next to the white window
half in the white light,
what can I say now, love love, cherish me?
Twin our mouths,
a perfect semblance?
Who touches stained glass holds one blue forearm,
one red elbow, yellow shoulder;
stay away, that vicious capacity shows itself
between the comic gestures; no perfume, no washing:
each morning two foam pillows mimic the texture,
the bedspread offers buds to play with middle fingers,
the language pours a storm against the stripped branches
lifting the sheet from the floor,
setting an imagined picture against the lamp base.
I stretch myself over each blue mountain.
A rainbow, one section, hung from a string that day.
One cotton bag hung from the low promising cloud
sways while I count each equation:
your smile where the scarring snips the wound free,
more open than any moon, any dark ring, crescent, visible, invisible,
oh love:
let me.